Countries Around the World

Ireland

Melanie Waldron

www.raintreepublishers.co.uk
Visit our website to find out more information about Raintree books.

To order:
☎ Phone 0845 6044371
▤ Fax +44 (0) 1865 312263
▨ Email myorders@raintreepublishers.co.uk

Customers from outside the UK please telephone +44 1865 312262

Raintree is an imprint of Capstone Global Library Limited, a company incorporated in England and Wales having its registered office at 7 Pilgrim Street, London, EC4V 6LB – Registered company number: 6695582

Edited by Laura Knowles
Designed by Victoria Allen
Original illustrations © Capstone Global Library Ltd 2012
Illustrated by Oxford Designers and Illustrators
Picture research by Mica Brancic
Originated by Capstone Global Library
Printed and bound in China by CTPS

ISBN 978 1 406 23577 7 (hardback)
15 14 13 12 11
10 9 8 7 6 5 4 3 2 1

ISBN 978 1 406 23584 5 (paperback)
16 15 14 13 12
10 9 8 7 6 5 4 3 2 1

British Library Cataloguing in Publication Data
Waldron, Melanie.
Ireland. -- (Countries around the world)
941.5'0824-dc22
A full catalogue record for this book is available from the British Library.

Acknowledgements
We would like to thank the following for permission to reproduce photographs: Alamy pp. **9** (© Sue Heaton), **15** (© Ros Drinkwater), **17** (© Kevin Schafer), **27** (© George Munday), **31** (© Imagestate Media Partners Limited - Impact Photos/Geray Sweeney), **33** (© Michael Cullen); Corbis pp. **10** (© Bettmann), **32** (© Bob King), **34** (© Marco Cristofori); Getty Images p. **7** (Hulton Archive); iStockphoto pp. **21** (© Tomas Bercic), **35** (© Andreas Kaspar), **39** (© ooyoo); Photolibrary pp. **25** (Hemis/Bertrand Rieger), **28** (Britain on View/Daniel Bosworth), **29** (Practical Pictures/ Craig Robertson); Shutterstock pp. **5** (© Walshphotos), **6** (© John Sones), **13** (© Stephen Bonk), **16** (© Hans Kwaspen), **18** (© Michael Steden), **19** (© Sue Robinson), **23** (© PHB.cz (Richard Semik)), **30** (© Eireann), **37** (© Andreas Juergensmeier), **46** (© Christophe Testi).

Cover photograph of Clare Island, County Mayo, Ireland reproduced with permission of Getty Images/Stone/ Travelpix Ltd.

We would like to thank Pádraic Whyte and Clodagh Moynan for their invaluable help in the preparation of this book.

Every effort has been made to contact copyright holders of material reproduced in this book. Any omissions will be rectified in subsequent printings if notice is given to the publishers.

Contents

Some words are printed in bold, **like this**. You can find out what they mean by looking in the glossary.

Introducing Ireland

Think of emeralds, and what do you imagine? Do you imagine lots of different colours of green? Ireland is sometimes known as "the emerald isle". This is because of the lush green vegetation that covers a lot of the country, creating a beautiful landscape.

Land of contrast

Ireland is a country with a very distinct **culture** and lots of old traditions. However, Ireland is also a modern, 21st-century country. Some modern developments have had a negative impact on Ireland's traditional culture, but others fit in well with it. This contrasting and surprising feel to the country draws tourists back again and again.

Ireland is an island, located in the northwest corner of Europe. It lies just to the west of Great Britain. Far to the west, across the Atlantic Ocean, lies Canada. The northeast corner of the island is part of the United Kingdom, and is called Northern Ireland. The rest of the island is called the Republic of Ireland, and is about a third of the size of the United Kingdom.

Ireland has had a troubled history, with violent clashes during its struggle for **independence** from the United Kingdom. However, Irish people have never lost their deep sense of culture and pride in their country. Towards the end of the 20th century, Ireland modernized very quickly. It became one of the richest countries in Europe. However, this was not to last.

The many different shades of green, shown here in the Vale of Glendasan, have helped Ireland get its nickname "the emerald isle".

History: turbulent times

Around 10,000 years ago, a huge ice sheet that had covered Ireland began to melt. From this time, people began to settle on the land. Evidence of these early **settlers** still remains today. For example, at Newgrange there is a **burial chamber** dating from around 3200 BC. It is a huge grass-covered dome, with a ring of white stone forming the walls. The entrance passage leads to the burial chamber. Every year, during the winter solstice (shortest day), the Sun shines straight along the passage and into the chamber.

The Celts and the Christians

Celts from Central Europe arrived in Ireland between the 8th and 3rd centuries BC. They organized the land into territories, each controlled by leaders, also known as chieftains. They also set up a basic code of law which was used until the 17th century. Traditional Celtic designs also came from these early settlers. **Christianity** arrived in Ireland between the 3rd and 5th centuries AD.

Traditional Celtic designs can be seen all over Ireland, for example in this Celtic stone cross.

SAINT PATRICK

Saint Patrick, who lived during the 4th and 5th centuries AD, is Ireland's **patron saint**, even though he actually came from Britain! He came to Ireland when he was 16, as a slave captured by Irish raiders. Here he found religion, before escaping and returning to Britain. He vowed to convert Ireland to Christianity, and within 30 years of his return to the country, most Irish people were Christians.

Early Christian monks created the Book of Kells in about AD 800. It is famous for its beautiful images that illustrate the four gospels of the New Testament.

The Vikings arrive

The Vikings first landed in Ireland in AD 795. At first they attacked settlements and raided **monasteries**, taking money and goods. Later they founded many of Ireland's towns, and eventually settled and mixed with the Celts.

The start of occupation

During the 1100s, the first English **nobles** (lords) arrived in Ireland, but their power and influence was mostly limited to the area around Dublin. However, in the 1530s the **Protestant** King of England, Henry VIII, took over the country. He declared himself King of Ireland in 1541. Elizabeth I and then James I took land away from the Irish through the **policy** of plantation. This meant forcing Irish landowners, who were **Catholics**, to give their land to Protestants from England and Scotland.

During the English Civil War (1642–1651) the Protestant Oliver Cromwell led invasions against Catholic groups in Ireland, to prevent them from siding against the Protestant **parliament** in England. There were **massacres** in the towns of Drogheda and Wexford, and by the end of Cromwell's campaign, 25 per cent of Ireland had been taken by Protestants.

Daily life

In 1695, the English introduced laws that had a terrible effect on Irish people. Catholics were not allowed to own land or to hold jobs with any power. The laws banned Irish culture, music, and education. To get round these laws, some Catholics became Protestant. More and more land was taken from Catholics and by the end of the 18th century, Catholics owned only five per cent of land throughout the country.

The potato famine

Between 1845 and 1851, Ireland was devastated by a terrible **famine**. A disease wiped out all the potato crops, a main food source at the time. At the same time, some other foods were being exported abroad by people keen to make money. Around one million people died and up to two million people **emigrated** (left the country) to go to the United States and Canada.

This memorial in Dublin reminds people of the Irish potato famine, and all the people who died or left the country during this sad time in Irish history.

The Irish fight back

By the 1900s, many Irish people wanted some kind of **independence** from the United Kingdom. On Easter Monday in 1916, a group made up of **nationalists**, **socialists** and members of the Women's League led a rebellion in Dublin. They declared Ireland independent. However, the British overcame the rebels and dealt with them very harshly. Fifteen of them were killed, and this led to a huge increase in support for an independent Ireland.

Two years later, the **republican** political party Sinn Féin (pronounced "Shin Feyn") won the most votes in the general **election**, and declared Ireland independent. Eventually, after agreeing a **treaty** with the British, the Irish Free State was created in 1922. The treaty stated that six counties in the north would remain part of the United Kingdom, and be known as Northern Ireland. Full independence was gained in 1948 when Ireland left the **British Commonwealth** and the Republic of Ireland was born.

The rebellion in 1916, known as the Easter Rising, left behind scenes of devastation in Dublin after the British fought back.

The Troubles

During the second half of the 1900s, Northern Ireland experienced a period of conflict that became known as "The Troubles". This lasted for more than 40 years. There were a number of reasons for the violence. One reason was that many people wanted Catholics and Protestants to be treated as equals in society. While some people organized peaceful protest marches, others resorted to violence. Another reason was that some people did not want Northern Ireland to be part of the United Kingdom, while others did. The violence led to more than 3,000 deaths.

In 1998, the Good Friday Agreement (also known as The Belfast Agreement) was signed by British, Irish, and Northern Irish politicians. It went a long way to establishing peace and a fairer political system.

Modern Ireland

In 1973, Ireland joined the EEC (which then became the **European Union (EU)**). Since then there has been a lot of **investment** in the country and, by the year 2000, Ireland was one of the wealthiest countries in Europe. In 2008 however, events in the Irish and global **economies** had a terrible impact in Ireland. Banks collapsed, businesses shut down, and unemployment rocketed. Even after accepting a large loan from the EU and the **International Monetary Fund (IMF)**, it will take Ireland many years to recover from these economic difficulties.

How to say...

English and Irish (Gaeilge) are both official languages in Ireland. English is used by the majority of the population. Irish is still spoken every day in some of the smaller villages in the west of Ireland. Here are a few words in Irish:

hello	*dia duit*	(djia dittch)
goodbye	*slán leat*	(slawn latt)
welcome	*fáilte*	(fall-cha)

Regions and resources: landscape and economy

Ireland is on the northwest edge of Europe. There are many different landscapes and **habitats** across the island.

The southeast corner of Ireland has gentle rolling hills, lush farmland and the warmest climate across Ireland. There are golden sandy beaches along the coast. There are also some ancient cities and towns, such as Waterford and Wexford, both founded by the Vikings.

Heading to the southwest corner, the coastline turns more jagged and rough, with rocky headlands meeting the Atlantic Ocean and a scattering of rocky islands along the coast. Huge expanses of white sand contrast with the high mountains in this area. Further inland, green valleys and rolling farmland dominate the landscape, with towns and villages dotted throughout.

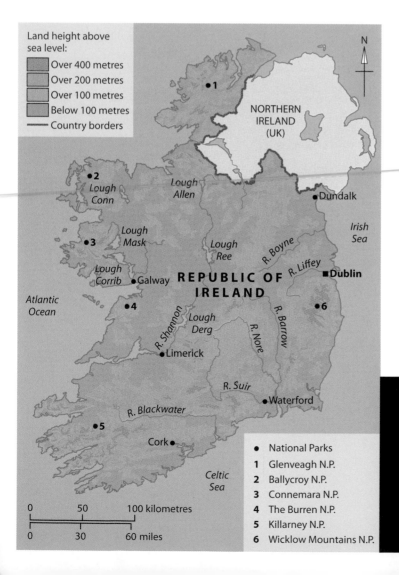

Land height above sea level:
- Over 400 metres
- Over 200 metres
- Over 100 metres
- Below 100 metres
- Country borders

NORTHERN IRELAND (UK)

•1

•2
Lough Conn
Lough Allen
•Dundalk

Lough Mask
•3
Lough Ree
R. Boyne
Irish Sea

Lough Corrib •Galway
REPUBLIC OF IRELAND
R. Liffey
■Dublin

Atlantic Ocean
•4
R. Shannon
Lough Derg
R. Nore
R. Barrow
•6

•Limerick

R. Suir

R. Blackwater
•5
Cork•
•Waterford

Celtic Sea

| 0 | 50 | 100 kilometres |
| 0 | 30 | 60 miles |

• National Parks
1 Glenveagh N.P.
2 Ballycroy N.P.
3 Connemara N.P.
4 The Burren N.P.
5 Killarney N.P.
6 Wicklow Mountains N.P.

This map of Ireland shows the rugged west coast, the large areas of rolling land and the mountains and lakes which dot the country.

In the western part of Ireland, lakes and bogs can be found alongside farmland, wild mountains, and the cities of Galway and Limerick. Towards the coast is a huge limestone **plateau**, called the Burren. Here the exposed rock is cut by deep cracks called *grykes*, and below ground there are caves and tunnels carved by water.

The Cliffs of Moher, on Ireland's west coast, rise up to 214 metres (702 feet) out of the sea.

In the east of Ireland, outside Dublin, there are pastures, lakes, and **bogland**. To the south of Dublin, the Wicklow Mountains offer some beautiful scenery. Dublin itself is a huge, sprawling city, and there are many towns along the east coast where people live and then travel into Dublin to work.

A mild climate

The warm waters of the Atlantic Gulf Stream help to keep Ireland's climate mild. It is a **temperate maritime** climate, with mild winters and cool summers. In winter, daily temperatures are usually 4–8 °Celsius (39–46 °Fahrenheit), rising to 15–20 °Celsius (59–68 °Fahrenheit) in summer. The weather in Ireland is fairly wet, with rain falling on around 270 days every year.

Ireland's resources

Ireland's land is not only beautiful, but it is one of the country's biggest resources. The fertile soils make excellent grazing pastures for cows and sheep, and meat and dairy foods are produced. Crops such as potatoes, wheat, and sugar beet grow well. The land also contains some important **minerals** such as copper, lead, zinc, and gypsum, and these are mined for industrial use. The seas surrounding Ireland are rich in fish and seafood.

Ireland's industries

Fishing and farming are relatively small industries in modern Ireland but, along with **brewing**, they contribute to the large food industry. Mining and processing materials such as steel, lead, zinc, silver, and aluminium grew in the 20th century. Other heavy industries include machinery and railway-equipment **manufacturing**. Production of chemicals and medical drugs has grown, as well as software production, tourism, and other **service industries**, for example banking and insurance. Glass, crystal, and textiles are also made in Ireland.

During the early part of the 21st century, the property and construction industries grew rapidly. However, this came to a halt in 2008 when Ireland entered into **recession**. Banks and financial companies collapsed, and unemployment rose dramatically.

This pie chart shows the proportion of people employed in different sectors of industry in Ireland. The figures are from 2010.

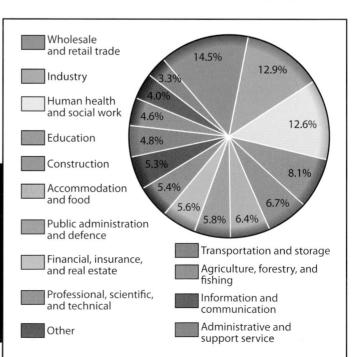

Wholesale and retail trade — 14.5%
Industry — 12.9%
Human health and social work
Education
Construction
Accommodation and food
Public administration and defence
Financial, insurance, and real estate
Professional, scientific, and technical
Other
Transportation and storage
Agriculture, forestry, and fishing
Information and communication
Administrative and support service

3.3%
4.0%
4.6%
4.8%
5.3%
5.4%
5.6%
5.8%
6.4%
6.7%
8.1%
12.6%

When the construction industry came to a crashing halt in the 2008 recession, many unfinished "ghost" housing estates were left across the country.

YOUNG PEOPLE

Most Irish school pupils have the chance to experience the world of work during work placements. Placements can be in any type of job, and students are encouraged to try one or two different jobs. This can really help them decide what type of career they would like to follow. Since the recession in 2008, jobs for young people are harder to find. Work placements can give students the valuable work experience they need to get a job later.

Wildlife: a varied environment

Ireland has many different **habitat** types, each providing a home for many different plants and animals.

Rocky coasts and islands

Along the western side of Ireland, much of the landscape is dominated by rocky headlands and cliffs. Here the vegetation is low-growing and tough, so it can survive in the thin soils and windy weather. Plants such as thrift and sea campion produce a beautiful spread of wild flowers in the summer. On many of the sea cliffs and rocky islands, huge colonies of sea birds can be found, such as gannets and choughs, which are now rare elsewhere.

The Burren

In the west of Ireland there is a huge area of limestone rock, called the Burren. In some places, the limestone is exposed and there are deep cracks in the rock, caused by water. This is known as a **limestone pavement**, and it has created a unique environment for plants. Mediterranean, arctic, and alpine plants all grow side by side here, including the hoary rock rose, which is very rare, and the beautiful spring gentian.

The Burren's wild flowers grow in the cracks running through the rock.

A range of habitats

Hedgerows and woodland provide good cover for many land mammals, for example foxes, badgers, rabbits, hedgehogs, shrews, pine martens, and Irish hares. In the remote hilly areas, herds of wild deer roam the land. Otters, seals, and dolphins can be spotted around the coast.

Ireland's position in the northwest corner of Europe makes it an ideal stop-over for birds **migrating** between North America and the Arctic, for example sandpipers and warblers. Birds from Africa migrate to Ireland in the spring, including shearwaters and corncrakes, which are in danger of dying out.

Gannets fly over the Skellig Islands, off the west coast of Ireland.

Bogs and mountains

Ireland has huge areas of bogland, covering around 13 per cent of the land. Sphagnum moss, bog rosemary, and black-beaked sedge grow well in the wet, acidic bog soil. There are also some **carnivorous** plants, such as the sundew, which traps insects with its sticky leaves. Some of Ireland's bogland has been destroyed due to cutting out **peat** for use as fuel. In the west of Ireland it is still possible to see wild Connemara ponies roaming the land.

Much of the hilly mountainous land is covered by heather. In the Wicklow Mountains in eastern Ireland, the beautiful peregrine falcon has been spotted, and in County Donegal there are some golden eagles.

Connemara ponies are strong and sturdy, calm and gentle, and make excellent riding ponies.

Wicklow Mountains National Park gives protection to the rare peregrine falcon.

Woodland

Very little ancient woodland can be found in Ireland today. Much of it was cleared by the British, especially during the time of Queen Elizabeth I. She wanted to expand England's Royal Navy and needed wood to build her ships. There are some small areas of original oak forest remaining, in Killarney National Park and in southern Wicklow. The rest of the woodland is mostly pine forest **plantations**, where only pine trees are planted, so the wood can later be sold.

Parks and reserves

Ireland has six national parks: the Burren, Connemara, Glenveagh, Killarney, Wicklow Mountains, and Ballycroy. These are shown on the map on page 12. In addition, there are 76 National Nature Reserves. There are also 12 forest parks, which cover 70 per cent of Ireland's forested areas. All of these areas will help to preserve the natural environment for years to come.

How to say...

limestone	*aolchloiche*	(ale-cli-ha)
mammal	*mamach*	(ma-mach)
otter	*dobharchú*	(dove-ar-coo)
peat	*móna*	(mow-na)
eagle	*iolair*	(il-arr)
forest	*foraoise*	(for-ae-sha)

Lakes and wetlands

Ireland's high rainfall and expanses of flat land have created large areas of lakes and wetlands. Here, waterfowl and waders fly in from the Arctic and Europe. The Wexford Wildfowl Reserve is home to half the world's population of Greenland white-fronted geese!

Ireland's rivers and lakes are generally very clean. However, in the past there has been some pollution due to agricultural and industrial waste, and untreated sewage running into the water. Some non-native species of water plant or animal have also been changing the environment. For example, the Zebra mussel was introduced to the River Shannon estuary in the 1990s. Since then it has been feeding on the **plankton** in the water that other native species would normally eat. Without enough food, many native species cannot survive.

Environmental issues

Like many modern countries, perhaps Ireland's biggest environmental issue is the increasing demand for energy, especially fossil fuels. Fossil fuels are coal, oil, and natural gas. They are used for energy, but can pollute the environment and cause global warming. In order to try and reduce the need for fossil fuels, 67 wind farms have been created to produce energy. Waste and pollution are other environmental issues facing Ireland, especially around the larger towns and cities.

Daily life

In order to help cut down on waste, shops in Ireland do not give out plastic bags for free. Each bag costs €0.22 (about 19 pence), and this has reduced their use by 90 per cent. So if you go shopping in Ireland, remember to take your own bags.

Wind farms across Ireland are producing energy and helping to reduce the demand for fuels.

Although tourism is good for Ireland's **economy**, so many tourists visit that they can often have a large impact on the environment. To combat this, **ecotourism** is being promoted, which includes encouraging people to visit places in a way that respects the environment. So in Ireland, tourists are encouraged to use public transport (or a bicycle) and eat locally-produced food. They are also encouraged to stay in guest houses and hotels that have good environmental practices, such as using **renewable** energy.

Infrastructure: Ireland's systems

There are three main political parties in Ireland – Fianna Fáil (feena fall), Fine Gael (finna gale), and Labour. **Elections** to the **parliament**, which is called the Oireachtas (ir–ochtas), take place every five years. The Oireachtas is at Leinster House in Dublin. There are two parts to the Oireachtas. The Dáil (dawl), or Lower House, has 166 members elected by the public. The Seanad (shanad), or Upper House, has 60 members elected by universities and nominated by the Taoiseach (tea–shoch). The Taoiseach is the Irish equivalent of a prime minister. He or she is the head of government. The Taoiseach's deputy is the Tánaiste (tawn-ishta).

Ireland also has a president, who fulfils certain roles as the head of the country. These roles include appointing members of the government and signing new **bills** passed by the government. The president also represents Ireland and the Irish people at some international events. Presidents are elected by the public every seven years.

This map shows the 26 counties of the Republic of Ireland and some of the main towns and cities.

This is Leinster House in Dublin, where the Irish parliament (Oireachtas) sits.

In January 2011, Ireland's prime minister, Brian Cowen, announced that a general election would take place in February 2011. This was a year earlier than the usual five-year term. Many people had called for an early election because of Ireland's economic crisis. They believed that Cowen's government, a **coalition** of Fianna Fáil, the Green Party and some independent politicians, had made too many mistakes. In February 2011, a new government was formed out of a coalition between Fine Gael and the Labour Party.

MARY McALEESE   (BORN 1951)

Mary McAleese was President of Ireland from 1997 until 2011. She was born in Belfast, in Northern Ireland. Before entering politics Mary worked as a journalist and a barrister (a type of lawyer). The president before her, Mary Robinson, was Ireland's first female president.

Education

Education is highly valued in Ireland and has been a priority for Irish governments for many years. It has a worldwide reputation for excellence and the attendance rates are among the highest in the world. The **literacy rate** in Ireland is 99 per cent. Education is **compulsory** between the ages of six and sixteen. The school year runs from September until the end of June.

Primary schools

Children attend primary school from age four or five to eleven or twelve. There are several key areas of study: languages (both Irish and English); mathematics; social, environmental, and scientific education (includes history and geography); arts education (includes visual arts, music, and drama); physical education; and social, personal, and health education.

Most primary schools teach subjects in English, but there are some schools, known as *gaelscoileanna*, which teach all subjects through the Irish language. Some schools have a uniform, others do not. Pupils can take part in a range of after-school activities, for example music, art, dance, and sport.

YOUNG PEOPLE

The Ark, in Dublin, claims to be Europe's first custom-built children's cultural centre. It runs events based on music, craft, literature, and theatre. The programme is developed with children, for children, and about children. Many school groups attend throughout term-time.

Post-primary education

Pupils aged 12 to 18 attend secondary schools, or post-primary schools. The first three years are the Junior Cycle, followed by a Transition Year and then the Senior Cycle. Irish, English, and maths are compulsory in all schools.

Island schools

Some of the islands off the coast of Ireland have small primary schools. One of the smallest is St Columba's School on Inishturk, an island off the west coast of County Galway. In 2010 there were six pupils, quite a lot fewer than in 1888 when there were 30! As on many islands, a lot of people left during the 20th century to find work in towns on the mainland and to improve their living conditions.

These pupils are having a music lesson in their village school.

Travelling in Ireland

There is an extensive network of surfaced roads in Ireland. Major motorways and dual carriageways connect towns and cities such as Dublin, Cork, and Galway. In the more remote areas, roads are single track only. This can lead to big queues and delays during the peak tourist season, as most tourists hire cars to travel to these areas. There are good bus services which usually carry bikes free of charge, so you can travel onwards to places the bus does not go.

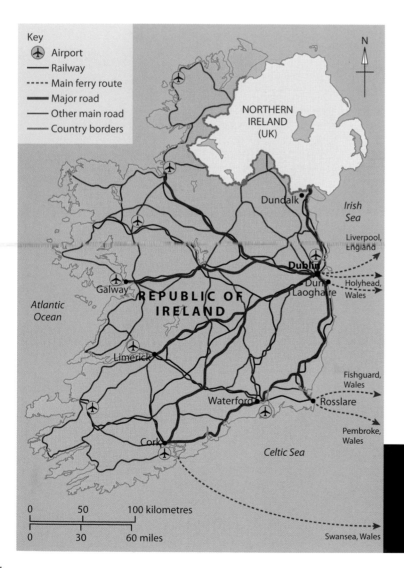

There are large international airports at Cork, Dublin, and Shannon, and several smaller airports providing mostly domestic flights. Ferry services connect islands and remote parts of the coastline, and also run across rivers, inlets, and lakes. These ferries provide welcome shortcuts for cyclists! There is also a train network which fans out from Dublin. However there are no train routes running north-to-south in the west of the island, and none at all in County Donegal!

Key
- ✈ Airport
- —— Railway
- ----- Main ferry route
- —— Major road
- —— Other main road
- —— Country borders

NORTHERN IRELAND (UK)

Dundalk

Irish Sea

Liverpool, England

Dublin

Dún Laoghaire

Holyhead, Wales

REPUBLIC OF IRELAND

Galway

Atlantic Ocean

Limerick

Fishguard, Wales

Waterford

Rosslare

Pembroke, Wales

Cork

Celtic Sea

Swansea, Wales

| 0 | 50 | 100 kilometres |
| 0 | 30 | 60 miles |

This map shows Ireland's main transport links.

This small vehicle ferry is crossing at Waterford harbour. There are many ferry services operating around Ireland's rugged coastline.

Healthcare in Ireland

Healthcare in Ireland is provided by the HSE (Health Service Executive). The HSE is funded by public **taxes**. Some medical charges are made to people who earn above a certain amount of money. Those who do not earn this amount receive Medical Cards. These allow people access to free services, such as visiting a doctor or staying in hospital, and reduced charges for prescriptions. Around half the population also has private health insurance. This means that they can usually see a consultant doctor more quickly, and they will probably get a private room if they need to stay in hospital.

Culture: Ireland's *craic*

Irish people are well known for having an easy-going nature and for being warm, friendly, and chatty. The word *craic* (pronounced "crack") is used to describe having fun or a good time. Traditionally, Irish family life was very close-knit. However, this is now becoming less common. As people move around the country or abroad for study and work, they spend less time in their local communities. In many remote areas though, the sense of community is still very strong.

Food and drink

Traditional Irish food is hearty and simple. However, new modern cuisine is now taking advantage of the good local Irish produce available. Meat, seafood, dairy products, and potatoes are staples of Irish cooking. In rural areas, lunch is usually the biggest meal of the day, while in urban areas, lunch tends to be smaller and quicker, with the main meal in the evening.

Some Irish specialities are:
- colcannon – mashed potato with cabbage and leeks
- Irish stew – lamb with potatoes, onions, and carrots
- black pudding – sausage made with pig's blood
- soda bread – light bread containing buttermilk and baking soda.

The clean seas of Ireland's west coast produce world-famous oysters. These are often enjoyed with a pint of Guinness.

In Ireland, people drink more tea per person than any other country! Everyone is quick to offer a cup to make visitors feel welcome. Another popular drink is a type of dark beer called stout. Guinness is a world-famous brand of Irish stout. Ireland also produces over 100 different types of whiskey (not whisky, which is made in Scotland!).

Champp

Ask an adult to help you make this delicious, warming dish.

Ingredients

- 100 grams spring onions, cut into rings
- 150 mililitres milk
- 900 grams potatoes
- 85–100 grams butter
- extra butter for serving

What to do

1. Put the spring onions and milk in a pan and heat until boiling, then remove from the heat.
2. Boil the potatoes in their skins for 30 to 40 minutes, until they are tender, then drain them. When they have cooled slightly, peel off the skins.
3. Mash the potatoes with the butter until there are no lumps left. Gradually stir in the milk and spring onions.
4. Season with a pinch of salt and pepper, and serve with a little knob of butter on top.

Religion

Around 87 per cent of the Irish population is registered as Roman **Catholic**, although many people do not actively practise the religion. Almost three per cent belong to the **Protestant** Church of Ireland. Other Christians make up almost two per cent of the population. Other religions make up around four per cent. Before the modernization of society in the mid-1900s, religion played a very big part in the lives of almost all Irish people. People would attend **Mass** in church several times a week. Now, however, it is mostly rural communities who attend regularly.

St Kevin's Church at Glendalough is typical of the many beautiful rural churches in Ireland.

Festivals

Throughout the year, Ireland has a huge programme of festivals across the country. Food, sport, arts, and local traditions are all represented at various festivals. The Dublin Horse Show happens in early August. This is a huge gathering, with people coming from outside Ireland to attend. The show features high-level showjumping competitions. For music lovers, the Cork Jazz Festival in late October is extremely popular. Perhaps the most important event is St Patrick's Day, on 17 March. On this day, many towns hold parades and **pilgrimages** to remember Ireland's **patron saint**.

At St Patrick's Day festivals across Ireland, dancing and dressing up are part of the celebrations.

Literature

Story-telling and poetry reading have always been popular pastimes. This tradition has helped Ireland to produce many great writers and poets. Oscar Wilde was a very famous playwright, poet, and novelist, known also for his flamboyant clothes. Bram Stoker, who wrote *Dracula*, and James Joyce, who wrote *Ulysses*, were also very famous. Modern Irish children's authors include Eoin Colfer, who wrote *Artemis Fowl*, and Siobhán Parkinson. In 2010, Dublin was designated a **UNESCO** City of Literature.

WILLIAM BUTLER YEATS (1865–1948)

Poet and dramatist W. B. Yeats was born in Dublin. When he was a child, he moved to London, England, but spent much of his school holidays visiting his grandparents in Sligo, in the west of Ireland. Along with other writers, he pushed forward the Irish Literary Revival in the early part of the 20th century. They wanted to keep Irish **culture** alive by writing about old stories and myths. Yeats died in France, and his body was later brought back to be buried in Sligo.

Music and dance

Traditional music is still very much part of Ireland's music scene. It has been kept alive because many modern musicians like to use traditional music with a modern slant. There are many different traditional instruments played in Ireland, such as the violin, tin whistle, flute, harp, banjo, *bodhrán* (a small goatskin drum), and the Uilleann pipes (similar to bagpipes).

There are also many traditional dances which accompany the music. For example, reels and jigs are both lively Irish dances. Traditional Irish dancing was given an enormous revival in the hugely successful Riverdance production, which has been shown all around the world.

Modern music

Ireland has produced one of the world's biggest rock bands – U2. Following them into the pop-music scene came, among others, The Pogues, Sinéad O'Connor, The Corrs, Boyzone, and Westlife.

Here, the Irish rock band U2 is playing to a huge audience in Sydney, Australia in 2010.

Sport

Most Irish people love sport – whether playing it or watching it! The Gaelic Athletic Association promotes traditional Irish sports, which are very popular in Ireland. In Gaelic football, the ball can be kicked or thrown. Hurling is a little like hockey, with a small ball moved using a stick. Camogie is very similar to hurling and is played by women only.

Rugby and football are very popular in Ireland, along with golf. Ireland also has a reputation for breeding world-class horses for racing and showjumping, which are also popular with many Irish people.

YOUNG PEOPLE

Ireland may not spring to mind as one of the best places in the world to surf, but in fact many locations along the west coast are ideal for this sport. However, a thick wetsuit is necessary in winter! The National Championships are held every April at Bundoran in County Donegal. Young people are encouraged to take part and compete in the Under-14 Championship.

The first official camogie match took place in 1904, and the sport has remained popular with Irish women ever since.

Ireland today

Ireland has come through many years of turbulence, but by the end of the 20th century, it was a modern, wealthy country. Irish people who had previously left Ireland to seek work and a good life elsewhere were now returning, along with new **immigrants**. Many of the immigrants came from Africa and Eastern Europe. Before the global economic crash of 2008, Ireland was given the nickname "Celtic Tiger", meaning that it was a strong and growing **economy**, with low unemployment and new wealth. When the **recession** began, immigration slowed and **emigration** increased once again.

The economic crash hit Ireland very hard. Banks collapsed, and the government spent a lot of money helping the banks out. Many people became unemployed. The government eventually agreed to accept a loan of €85 billion, mostly from the **EU** and the **IMF**. However, the government also had to agree to impose tax rises and spending cuts, seriously affecting the Irish people. Ireland is now slowly starting to recover.

Ireland's capital, Dublin, is a busy city that mixes modern business with its rich culture and history.

Ireland's beautiful scenery and varied list of activities available will draw visitors back to the country again and again.

The upside

Despite the recent financial problems, the Irish people still have much to be proud of. There are some excellent systems in place to help safeguard the quality of life for the Irish. Ireland has good transport and communication links across the country, everyone has access to healthcare, and there is an excellent education system with high **literacy rates** and many people enter further education after leaving school.

There are also some aspects of Ireland that economic problems can never change, and which will remain part of Irish society for many years to come. The amazing scenery and varied wildlife will continue, as will the deeply-rooted sense of **culture**, and of course, the *craic*! If you visit Ireland, you will find plenty to do, from attending festivals and visiting museums and theatres, to walking, climbing, cycling, kayaking, windsurfing, horse riding, fishing, and bird-watching.

Fact file

Official name:	Ireland
Official languages:	English and Irish (Gaeilge)
Capital city:	Dublin
Bordering countries:	Northern Ireland (part of the United Kingdom)
Land area:	70,273 square kilometres (27,133 square miles)
Population:	4,670,976 (2011 estimate)
Largest cities and populations:	• Dublin (506,211 people)
	• Cork (119,418 people)
	• Galway (72,414 people)
	• Limerick (52,539 people)
Birth rate:	16.1 births per 1,000 people (2011 estimate)
Death rate:	6.34 deaths per 1,000 people (2011 estimate)

This pie chart shows the proportion of different religions practised in Ireland.

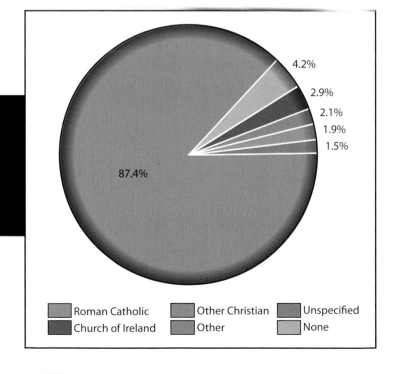

4.2%
2.9%
2.1%
1.9%
1.5%
87.4%

Roman Catholic Other Christian Unspecified
Church of Ireland Other None

Unemployment rate: 13.7 per cent (2010 estimate)

Type of government: parliamentary democracy

Independence date: 6 December 1921

World Heritage sites: Skellig Michael and Brugh na Boìnne

The monastery buildings on Skellig Michael, off the south-west coast of Ireland, date back to the 7th century. The island is so remote and rarely visited that the ruins are incredibly well preserved.

Climate: temperate maritime, modified by North Atlantic Current; mild winters, cool summers, consistently humid, overcast about half the time

This chart shows the average temperature, sunshine, and rainfall in Ireland.

	Jan	Feb	Mar	Apr	May	Jun	July	Aug	Sep	Oct	Nov	Dec
Average daily temperature (degrees Celsius)	4.6	4.8	6.1	7.9	10.4	13.2	14.9	14.6	12.6	10.1	6.4	5.4
Average daily hours of sunshine	1.6	2.3	3.1	4.6	5.3	4.8	4.2	4.2	3.6	2.7	2.0	1.4
Average monthly rainfall (mm)	76	54	61	53	61	56	59	78	71	84	74	78

Highest point: Carrauntoohil 1,041 metres (3,415 feet)

Coastline length: 1,448 kilometres (900 miles)

Longest river: River Shannon, 386 kilometres (240 miles)

Biggest lake Lough Corrib, 200 square kilometres (77 square miles)

Natural resources natural gas, peat, copper, lead, zinc, silver, barite, gypsum, limestone, dolomite

Currency: euro (€)

Major industries: mining, food products, brewing, textiles, clothing, chemicals, pharmaceuticals, machinery, rail-transportation equipment, glass and crystal, software, tourism

Imports:	data-processing equipment, other machinery and equipment, chemicals, petroleum and petroleum products, textiles, clothing
Exports:	machinery and equipment, computers, chemicals, pharmaceuticals, live animals, animal products
Public holidays:	New Year's Day (1 Jan) St Patrick's Day (17 March) Easter (Good Friday, EasterMonday) May Holiday (first Monday in May) June Holiday (first Monday in June) August Holiday (first Monday in August) October Holiday (last Monday in October) Christmas Day (25 December) St Stephen's Day (26 December)
National anthem:	Amhrán na bhFiann (The Soldiers' Song)
National symbols:	shamrock (three-leaved clover), Celtic cross, Celtic harp, Claddagh ring

The shamrock, with its three leaves, is a well-known symbol of Ireland.

Timeline

BC is short for "before Christ". BC is added after a date and means that the date occurred before the birth of Jesus Christ, for example, 450 BC.

AD is short for *Anno Domini*, which is Latin for "in the year of our Lord". AD is added before a date and means that the date occurred after the birth of Jesus Christ, for example, AD 720.

3200 BC	Newgrange **burial chamber** is built
8th–3rd century BC	**Celts** arrive from Central Europe
3rd–5th century AD	**Christianity** arrives in Ireland
4th–5th century AD	St Patrick converts Irish people to Christianity
AD 795	The Vikings arrive in Ireland
AD 800	The Book of Kells is created
1100s	English **nobles** arrive in Dublin
1530s	King Henry VIII of England takes over Ireland
1541	Henry VIII declares himself King of Ireland
1642–1651	The English Civil War is faught. During this, Oliver Cromwell leads invasions in Ireland against **Catholic** groups, to prevent them from siding against the **Protestant parliament** in England
1695	English laws imposed on Irish people stop them from owning their own land or have powerful jobs. Irish **culture**, music, and education are banned.

1845–1851	The potato **famine** sweeps across Ireland. Around one million people died and another two million people left Ireland
1904	The first official camogie match takes place, and the sport becomes popular among Irish women
1916	Irish rebellion against British rule in Dublin
1922	The Irish Free State is created, following the Anglo-Irish **Treaty** on 6 December 1921
1948	The Republic of Ireland gains full **independence**
late 1900s	The Troubles lead to over 3,000 deaths
1973	Ireland joins the EEC (later known as the **EU**)
1998	The Good Friday Agreement, or Belfast Agreement, is signed to signal an end to The Troubles
2008	The global economic crash affects Ireland
July 2010	Dublin is designated a **UNESCO** City of Literature – one of only four in the world
December 2010	The Irish government accepts a huge loan from the EU and the **IMF**
February 2011	Following a general **election**, a new **coalition** government is formed between Fine Gael and Labour

Glossary

bill law that has been suggested

bogland wet area with soil that is made up of decayed plants

brewing making alcoholic drinks such as beer

British Commonwealth group of countries that were once part of the British Empire

burial chamber specially created room where someone's body is put after death

carnivorous eating other animals

Catholic relating to a branch of Christianity which is led by the Pope

Celts group of people living in Britain and Ireland before Roman times; the Celts started coming to Britain and Ireland from Europe in the 8th century BC

Christianity religion based on the teachings of Jesus Christ

coalition government made up of two or more political parties working together

compulsory necessary, required or demanded

culture practices, traditions, and beliefs of a society

economy relating to the money, industry, and jobs in a country

ecotourism travelling to or visiting places in a way that respects the environment

election when the public votes on who will represent them in parliament

emigrate leave one country to live in another

European Union (EU) international organization of European countries with shared political and economic aims. The EU formed from the EEC (European Economic Community) in 1993.

famine large-scale lack of food over a wide area

habitat environment where a plant or animal is found

International Monetary Fund (IMF) organization of 187 countries that promotes international trade and financial stability

immigrant person who has moved to another country and settled there

independence having freedom from outside control

investment putting money into something for the purpose of making more money

limestone pavement area of flat limestone where cracks have formed

literacy rate percentage of people in a country who can read and write

manufacturing making things in large quantities using machines

Mass religious ceremony in the Roman Catholic Church

massacre killing a large number of people

migrate change habitat or location, usually when the seasons change

mineral substance formed naturally in rocks and earth

monastery building used by a community of monks

nationalist someone who wants his or her country to have its own government

noble person of high rank or title

parliament group of people who make the laws for a country

patron saint saint regarded as the special guardian of a country

peat plant remains that have partly rotted in bogs and other wetlands. Peat is used as fuel, and in farming and gardening.

pilgrimage trip to a religious place

plankton microscopic (very small) plants and animals floating in water

plantation large area of land where one type of plant is grown to sell

plateau wide, flat area of land that is higher than the land around it

policy set of rules or plans that is used as a guide for action

Protestant relating to a branch of Christianity which is separate from the Catholic or Orthodox church

recession period of economic decline

renewable able to be used over and over again without any loss of resources

republican belonging to a republic or wanting your country to be a republic. A republic is ruled by an elected government and president, and does not have a king or queen

service industry jobs that are involved with providing knowledge and time to help others

settler person who settles in a new area

socialist someone who believes that a country's main industries should be owned by the government, not by individual people

tax money paid by people to the government. Taxes can come from wages or be placed on goods that people buy.

temperate maritime type of climate that is cooler in winter and warmer in summer, and weather is affected by the ocean currents

treaty formal agreement between two or more countries

UNESCO stands for United Nations Educational, Scientific, and Cultural Organization. One of UNESCO's aims is to build peace and communication between different cultures.

Find out more

Books

Gruesome Guides: Dublin (Horrible Histories), Terry Deary (Scholastic, 2010)

Ireland (Countries of the World), Anna McQuinn and Colm McQuinn
(National Geographic, 2008)

Ireland (Horrible Histories Special), Terry Deary (Scholastic, 2009)

Ireland: In the Children's Own Words (Our Lives, Our World), Susie Brooks
(Chrysalis, 2005)

Tales from Old Ireland, Malachy Doyle and Naimh Sharkey
(Barefoot Books, 2005)

The Story of Ireland, Brendan O'Brien (O'Brien Press, 2009)

Websites

www.discoverireland.com

The official website of Tourism Ireland, an agency responsible for marketing
Ireland all around the world. Visit this site for information about Ireland
and Irish people, and some good places to visit and stay.

www.discoverireland.ie

This website is operated by Fáilte Ireland, the National Tourism Development
Authority. It has lots of information about accommodation, activities, events,
tourist attractions, and food.

www.greenbox.ie

Go to this site for information about visiting the "greenbox" area in the north
of Ireland, promoted as "Ireland's first ecotourism destination". Low-impact
accommodation and activities are listed, as well as tips on making your
whole visit more eco-friendly.

DVDs

Into the West (Cinema Club, 2003)
The Secret of Kells (Walt Disney, 2009)
The Secret of Roan Inish (Cinema Club, 2007)
Westlife: Live at Croke Park (SonyBMG, 2008)

Places to visit

The Ark
11a Eustace Street
Temple Bar, Dublin 2
www.ark.ie
This is a children's cultural centre in Dublin. There is a programme of craft, music, literature, and theatre activities for children.

Brú na Bóinne
Donore
County Meath
www.meath.ie/Tourism/Heritage/HeritageSites/Newgrange
The ancient burial sites of the early settlers on Ireland are among the oldest in Europe. The visit starts at the visitor centre, from where shuttle buses take you to visit the tombs.

Irish National Heritage Park
Ferrycarrig
County Wexford
www.inhp.com
Here, 9,000 years of Irish history are squashed into one visit! There are recreations of ancient farmsteads, shipyards, and forts, with costumed guides to help take you back to the past.

Topic tools

You can use these topic tools for your school projects. Trace the map on to a sheet of paper, using the black outline to guide you.

The Irish flag has three coloured rectangles. Green represents the mostly Catholic native people of Ireland. Orange represents the mostly Protestant settlers who came to Ireland from the 12th century onwards. White represents peace between these two groups in Ireland. Copy the flag design and then colour in your picture. Make sure you use the right colours!

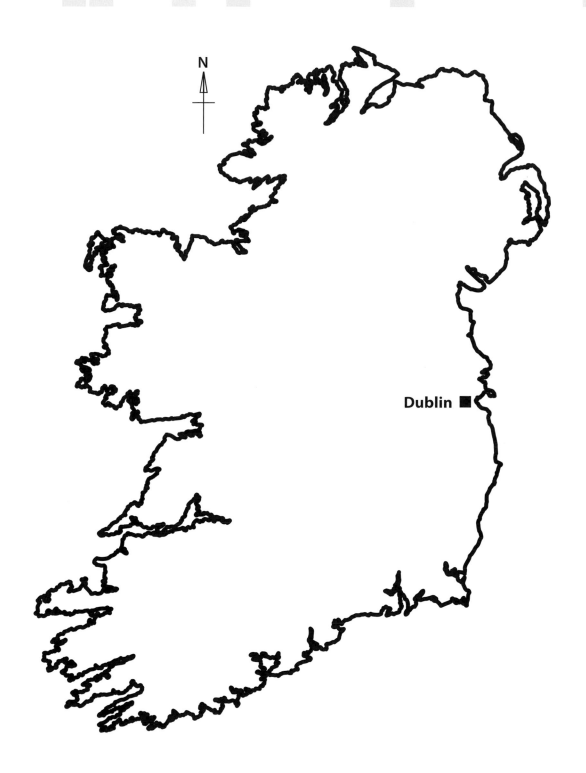

N

Dublin ■

Index